Country and City

Written by Amy White
Illustrated by Hector Cuenca

I live on a farm in the country.

I live in an apartment in the city.

A rooster wakes me up in the morning.

An alarm clock wakes me up in the morning.

I eat eggs from our chickens for breakfast.

I eat cereal and fruit for breakfast.

I feed the chickens before school.

I feed my fish before school.

I ride the bus to school.

I walk to school.

I do my homework at the kitchen table.
So do I.

I like to ride my bike.
So do I.

I like to watch movies.
So do I.

I like to swim.
So do I.

We are different, but we are also the same.